knitting for beginners

by Jessie Rubenstone

Photographs by Edward Stevenson

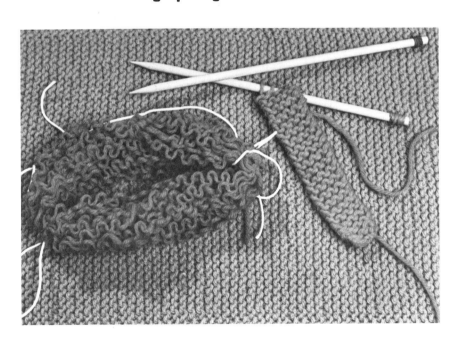

J. B. Lippincott Company / Philadelphia and New York

U.S. Library of Congress Cataloging in Publication Data

Rubenstone, Jessie.
  Knitting for beginners.

  SUMMARY: Explains the use of appropriate materials and techniques
for knitting headbands, belts, scarves, afghans, and other articles.
  1. Knitting — Juvenile literature. [1. Knitting] I. Title.
TT820.R78   746.4'3   73-6755
ISBN-0-397-31473-6 (reinforced bdg.)   ISBN-0-397-31474-4 (pbk.)

To Joan and David,

Jeffrey and Debbie,

Julia and Susan.

contents

so you want to knit

Knitting is fun. Knitting is work. Put these two together and you have a fun thing to do that will give you something worthwhile.

Hand-knitted articles are different from those that are knitted by machine, and cost more when bought in a store. Hand knits wear better, wash better, and last longer. It is easier to get just what you want when you make something yourself. You can pick the color and style, and the cost is much less. Also, the wool can be ripped, or unraveled, and used again (recycled).

So what is knitting? Knitting is pulling one long continuous piece of yarn through loops to form a fabric. Knitting needles are used to pull the yarn through the loops. In this book you will find directions for the basic stitches—knitting and purling—and instructions for some easy projects using these stitches. You may want to ask someone who knows how to knit to help you follow these directions. With the skills you will develop, you will be able to make the more advanced projects you will find in other books.

The first thing you will knit will be a sample. Practice making your sample until it is right. Do not expect your knitting to look perfect. Only machine knitting is perfect.

At first knitting may seem very hard to do, but as you practice you will find that it gets much easier, and later you will really enjoy it. You will find that you can knit while talking with friends or listening to the radio.

what you will need

The two things you will need in order to knit are *knitting needles* and *yarn*. They may be bought in department stores, five-and-ten-cent stores, and knitting shops.

KNITTING NEEDLES

Knitting needles come in pairs and are made of plastic, metal, or wood. They come in different lengths and different sizes (thicknesses). The number on the end of the needle shows the size. The bigger the number, the thicker the needle. When you knit with a large-size needle your knitting will be looser than if you use a smaller one.

Knitting needles cost about fifty cents to a dollar, depending on the size. They should last a lifetime. If a plastic or wooden needle breaks, you can put a new point on it with a pencil sharpener.

The knitting needles that were used to make the things in this book are size 10½. The "do-it-yourself" needles shown on page 14 are also size 10½. If you use a smaller needle and follow the same directions, your knitting will be tighter and the finished article smaller than the size given.

YARN

Yarn is made by twisting fibers (wool, cotton, synthetic, etc.) together into threads. This process is called *spinning*. These thin threads (or strands) are then twisted together to form thread that is heavy enough for knitting. The thin thread is called *ply* and the heavy thread is called *yarn*.

The number of ply tells how heavy the yarn is. In the picture you will see that the thin yarn is three-ply (has three strands) and the heavy yarn is four-ply (has four strands). It is easy to untwist an end of yarn and count the strands.

Yarn is sold in skeins or balls. Read the label when you buy yarn. It will tell you:

The fiber the yarn is made of (wool, orlon, etc.).
The weight of the skein. This is given in ounces.
The ply (number of plies) of the yarn.
The number of the color and the number of the dye lot. A *dye lot* is a batch of yarn that is dyed at the same time. Buy all the yarn needed for the article at one time. Be sure the dye lot number is the same. Yarn from different dye lots will not match exactly even if the color may look the same.

The yarn used for all the projects in this book is four-ply yarn. This is a good weight to use when you start knitting. Although a four-ounce skein will probably cost around $1.30, you may be able to find it on sale for under a dollar. In the directions for making the articles in this book you will find the number of ounces of yarn you will need. You can see how much the yarn will cost before you begin your project.

Yarn does not have to be new. Used yarn can be made to look as good as new. If you have an old hand-knitted garment that can be ripped, follow the directions for ripping on page 15.

All the yarn does not need to be the same color. Two or more colors can be used to make stripes. If you use different yarns, make sure they are the same weight. Do not mix three-ply with four-ply yarn.

In addition to knitting needles and yarn you will also need:

A *crochet hook*. Crochet hooks may be made of plastic, metal, or wood. They come in different sizes. Any size may be used to add the fringe to knitted articles. The crochet hook may also be used to hide the ends of yarn by pulling them through nearby stitches.

A *tapestry needle*. This is a thick sewing needle with a large eye and a rounded point. It is used to sew knitting together. It is also used to hide ends of yarn by weaving them in and out of nearby stitches.

A *darning needle* may be used for this as it also has a large eye.

do-it-yourself materials

MAKING KNITTING NEEDLES FROM DOWELS

A dowel is a round wooden stick. You can buy it in a hardware store or lumberyard. Dowels come 36 inches long and are made in different thicknesses. Buy a quarter-inch dowel (this means that the dowel is 1/4 inch thick). It will cost about ten cents.

Your dowel will make three knitting needles. They will be about twelve inches long and size 10½. This is the size needle that is used in making the articles in this book. Two needles make a pair.

To make the needles, use a ruler to measure 12 inches from each end of the dowel. Mark these measurements with a pencil.

If you do not have a saw to cut through these two pieces, it is easy to break a dowel. Place the dowel on a table with one of the marks along the edge of the table. (Protect the table with newspapers.) Hold the dowel firmly on the table and break it by pressing down the end. Do the same at the other end. This will give you three sticks that are about twelve inches long.

Use the two end pieces for your pair of needles, as they have a straight end for the bottom of the needles. Sharpen the broken end with a pencil sharpener. Rub your needles lightly with extra fine sandpaper until they are smooth. (You can buy sandpaper in a five-and-ten or a hardware store. Buy one sheet of extra fine sandpaper. It should cost about five cents.) Be careful to get the points smooth, but not too sharp. You may also wax your needles by rubbing them with a piece of candle or any other kind of wax.

Wrap a rubber band around the bottom of each needle (the flat end) to keep the stitches from falling off. You now have a good pair of knitting needles, size 10½. Different size dowels may be used to make other size needles.

Recycled yarn, before (left) and after washing (right), and do-it-yourself needles.

RE-USING (RECYCLING) OLD YARN

If you have an old hand-knitted garment that is no longer used, you can take it apart and use the yarn over again. Only yarn from items that were knitted by hand can be used again.

TO RIP OR UNRAVEL: If the garment has been sewed together, carefully remove the stitches that hold the pieces together at the seams. Be careful not to cut the knitting as it will come apart in small pieces. Remember that knitting is one long continuous thread.

When there are no more seams, find the place where the end of the yarn was fastened. Pull this end of yarn, and when it is free it will unravel very easily (*a*). As you rip, wind the yarn loosely around the back of a chair.

When you come to the end of the yarn, or to a knot, stop and follow these instructions. Untie or cut the

(*a*)

knot. Tie a piece of string or yarn around each end of the skein. This will keep the yarn from getting tangled while you wash and dry it. Remove the yarn from the chair. Repeat until all of the yarn has been unraveled and tied into skeins.

Wash in cold water with mild detergent or soap. Rinse well in several changes of cold water, stretching the yarn to get out the wrinkles. *Do not squeeze out water.* Use the strings on the skeins to hang them *dripping wet* over the bathtub or on a clothesline. Keep yarn out of sun.

When the yarn is dry, put it back on the same chair. Remove the strings and roll the yarn loosely into balls. You now have clean yarn ready to knit.

making the sample

Before you start to knit any of the things in this book, be sure that you can make a good sample. Even if you feel sure that you can knit, you should follow the directions and make the sample. You may use any kind of yarn and any size needles. It is a good idea to practice on scrap yarn or even heavy string and save your good yarn for the article you plan to make.

LEFT-HANDED KNITTING: If you are left-handed, follow the instructions, but when it says "right hand" use the left hand, and when it says "left hand" use the right hand. Hold a mirror in front of the pictures and look into the mirror. This will give you the picture for left-handed knitting.

CASTING ON STITCHES

Before you can start to knit you will need to make a row of loops on your needle. This is called *casting on stitches*. Follow the directions under each picture and do one step at a time as shown. There are several ways to cast on stitches. This is the easiest way. Later, as you knit, you will learn other ways.

When you get the correct number of loops on your needle, you are ready to knit. For the sample, cast on sixteen stitches. Be sure the loops are loose enough to move easily along the needle.

1. Make a slip loop as shown and slide it onto one needle. Pull ends to close up loop only until it will slide easily along the needle. This loop is the first stitch.

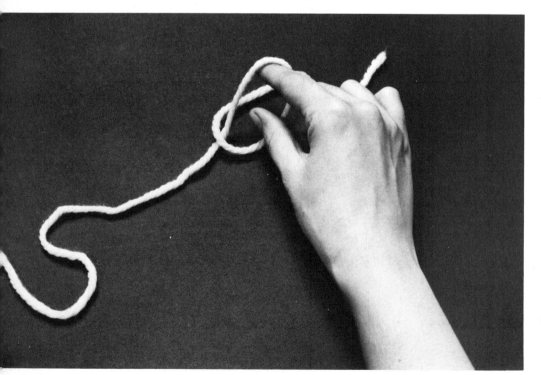

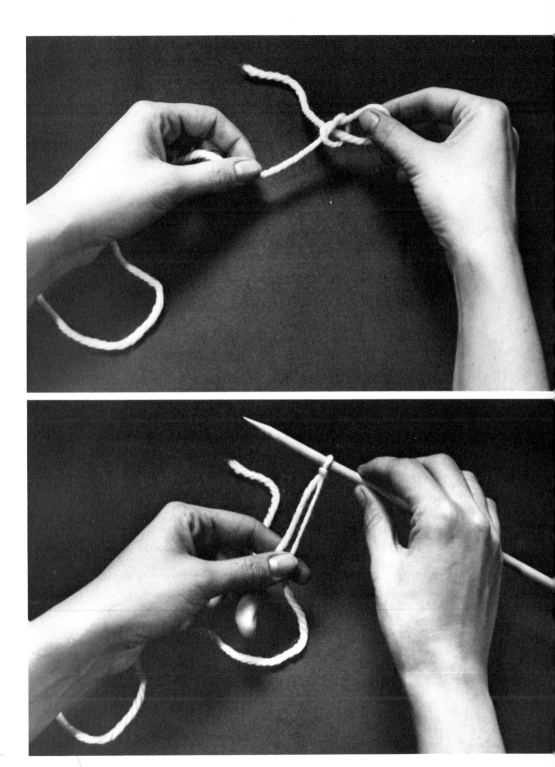

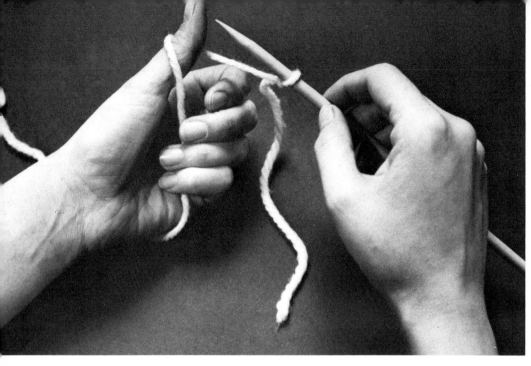

2. Holding needle in right hand, bring long end of yarn around left thumb as shown.

3. Slip end of needle *under* yarn at the front of your thumb. This will form a loop around the needle.

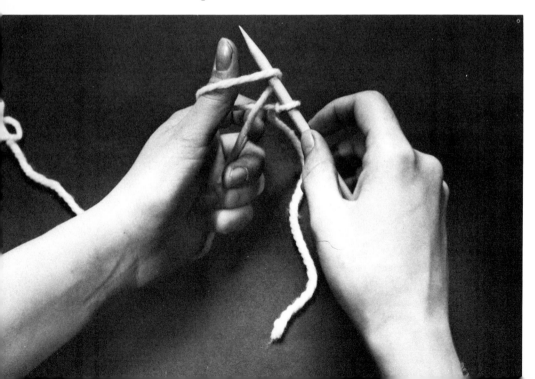

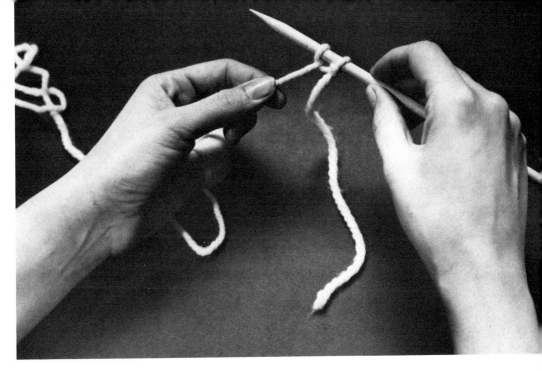

4. Pull long end of yarn to close up loop. You have cast on two stitches.

Repeat steps 2, 3, and 4 until you have cast on the right number of stitches.

HOW TO KNIT

Follow the directions under each picture and do one step at a time. Be sure to keep the stitches loose.

The rows are knitted back and forth. When you get to the end of the row, all the stitches will be on the right needle. Take the needle with the stitches in your left hand and turn it so the point is on your right. The empty needle is now the right needle. You are ready to knit the next row.

21

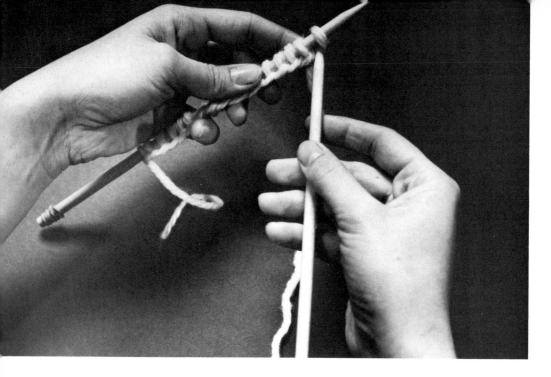

1. Hold the needle with the loops in your left hand (we will call this the left needle). Take the other needle in your right hand (we will call this the right needle). Put the right needle through the first loop from front to back. It should go in on the left side of the front of the loop and come out on the right side of the back of the loop.

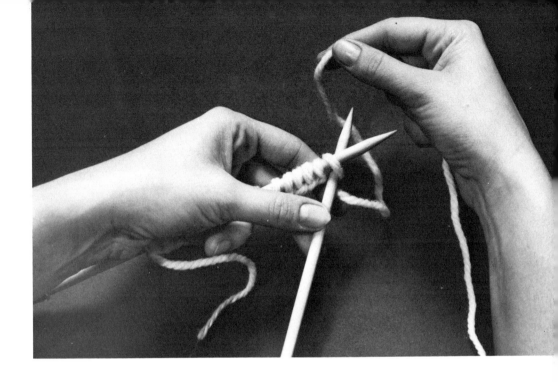

2. Using your right hand, pick up the yarn from the back and bring it under and around the right needle.

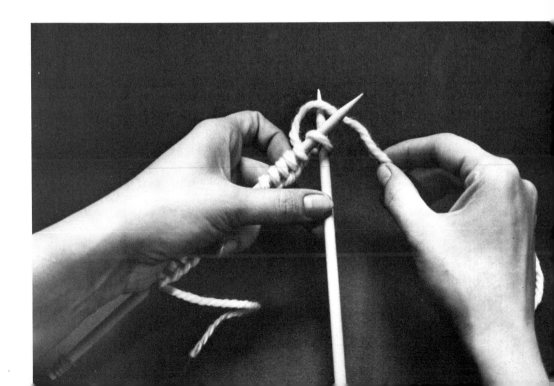

3. Hold both the yarn and the right needle with your right hand, pulling yarn firmly against right needle. Use the right needle to pull the yarn through the loop.

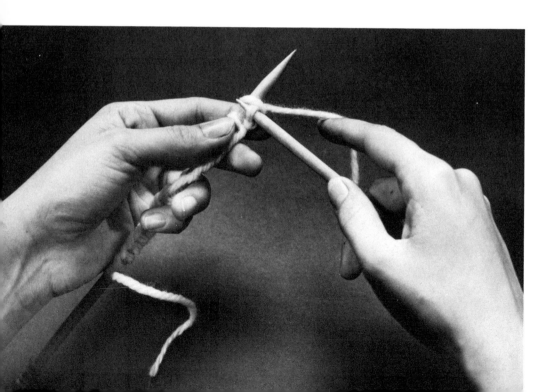

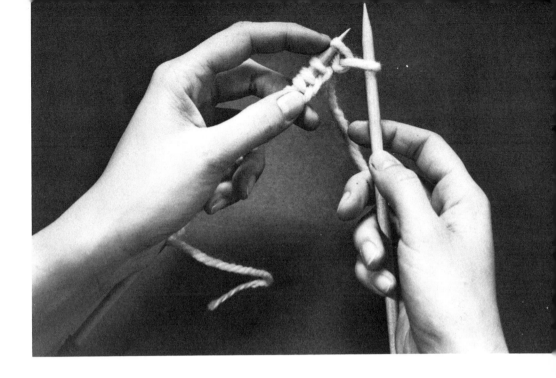

4. Slip the new stitch off the left needle. You have made the first stitch. Knit every loop until all the stitches are on the right needle.

Count your stitches at the end of each row. There must always be the same number. If you do not have the same number, you have made a mistake. If you have fewer than sixteen stitches you have dropped stitches, and if you have more than sixteen stitches you have added some. Keep practicing until you do not make any mistakes and you always have the same number of stitches at the end of each row.

This kind of knitting is called *knit stitch*. When you knit every stitch of every row, you will be doing a pattern called *garter stitch*. The other important stitch in knitting is called the *purl stitch*. You will learn to purl further along in this book.

Measure the width of your sample. When measuring knitting, put your work on a flat surface, such as a table or the floor. Use a ruler, tape measure, or yardstick. *Do not stretch the knitting.* If you have used size $10^{1/2}$ needles, you will find that your sample is about $4^{1/2}$ inches wide. Make the sample into a square by continuing to knit until the length is the same. You are now ready to bind off the stitches.

BINDING OFF STITCHES

Taking stitches off the needle to end a piece of knitting is called *binding off* or *casting off*. Follow directions under each picture and do one step at a time. As you bind off, keep the stitches *very loose*.

You have now made your sample. Now that you can knit, you will be able to follow the directions for making the articles in this book.

1. Knit the first two stitches in the row.

2. Put point of left-hand needle into the front of *first* stitch on right-hand needle.

3. With point of left-hand needle, pull the first stitch over the second stitch and over the point of the right-hand needle so that it drops off, leaving one stitch on right-hand needle.

You have bound off one stitch. Knit next stitch.

Repeat steps 2 and 3 until only one stitch remains on right-hand needle.

4. Cut the yarn, leaving an end a few inches long. Pull the end through the loop of the last stitch to fasten.

abbreviations

An abbreviation is a short form of a word. Abbreviations are used in directions for knitting. In the directions for making the articles in this book, the following abbreviations are used:

in	inch
k	knit
oz	ounce or ounces
p	purl
st	stitch
sts	stitches

The directions for making the sample you have just completed would look like this:

SAMPLE SQUARE

Knitting needles	1 pair size 10½
Yarn	⅓ oz (4-ply)
Size	4½ in × 4½ in

Cast on 16 sts. K every row until the length of the piece measures the same as the width (about 4½ inches). Bind off.

articles to knit

HEADBAND

Knitting needles	1 pair size 10½
Yarn	¼ oz (4-ply)
Size	1¼ in × 13 in

Cast on 5 sts. K every row until piece measures 13 inches. (Do not stretch when measuring.) Bind off. Sew the two ends together.

Headband before (above) and after sewing (below).

TO SEW KNITTED ARTICLES TOGETHER: Pin the two edges together evenly. Thread a tapestry needle with the same yarn that was used in making the article. Do not put a knot in the yarn. Fasten the yarn well at the beginning of the seam by taking two or three stitches in the same place.

Work from side to side, taking small stitches in the edges from the underside, as shown. Try to keep the seam flat.

Fasten the yarn at the end of the seam by taking two or three stitches in the same place so that it does not show.

The sewing may be done on the right or wrong side.

SMALL BELT

Knitting needles	1 pair size 10½
Crochet hook	Any size
Yarn	½ oz (4-ply)
Size (including fringe)	1½ in × 40 in
Fringe	12 pieces of yarn, 6 inches long

Cut the yarn for the fringe before starting to knit the belt. Set the fringe aside until after the belt is knitted.

Cast on 6 sts. K every row until piece measures 35 inches. Bind off and add fringe.

Small belt (left) and large belt (right).

FRINGE: The fringe is pulled through the stitches at the short ends of the belt.

Put the crochet hook through the first stitch and

33

catch the center of the 6-inch piece of fringe (*a*). Pull it halfway through. This will form a loop (*b*). Put two fingers through this loop, grab the two ends of yarn, and pull through the loop. Pull tight (*c*). Repeat this for each stitch along both ends.

(*a*)

(b)

(c)

LARGE BELT

Knitting needles	1 pair size 10½
Crochet hook	Any size
Yarn	1 oz (4-ply)
Size (including fringe)	2 in × 54 in
Fringe	14 pieces of yarn, 9 inches long

Cast on 7 sts and k every row until piece measures 46 inches. Bind off and add fringe.

Beads may be put on the fringe if long (9-inch) fringe is used. Knot the fringe to hold the beads in place.

You can cut many pieces of fringe at a time by winding yarn around a piece of cardboard as in making a pompon (page 52).

Fringe may be arranged in different ways. Try two pieces of yarn in each stitch, or two or three pieces of yarn in every other stitch. Or the articles may be made without fringe.

SMALL SCARF

Knitting needles	1 pair size 10½
Crochet hook	Any size
Yarn	1 4-oz skein (4-ply)
Size (including fringe)	8½ in × 38 in
Fringe	60 pieces of yarn, 5 inches long

Cut the yarn for the fringe before starting to knit. Set this aside until after the scarf is knitted.

Cast on 30 sts. K every row until all the yarn has been used, leaving enough to bind off. Bind off. Follow directions for fringe on page 33.

Small scarf (left)
and large scarf
(right).

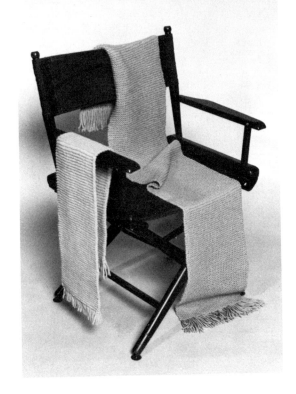

LARGE SCARF

Knitting needles	1 pair size 10½
Crochet hook	Any size
Yarn	2 4-oz skeins (4-ply)
Size (including fringe)	11 in × 68 in
Fringe	80 pieces of yarn, 7 inches long

Follow directions for small scarf, but cast on 40 sts. If you make the large scarf, you will have to join two pieces of yarn.

TO JOIN TWO PIECES OF YARN: Tie a firm knot. It is a good idea to tie the knot at the end of a row, where it will not show. Hide the ends of the knotted pieces by threading each end into a tapestry needle and weaving it in and out of a few stitches on the wrong side of the knitting. Or use a crochet hook to pull the ends of the yarn through nearby stitches.

SQUARES

Knitting needles	1 pair size 10½
Yarn	⅓ oz (4-ply)
Size	4½ in × 4½ in

Cast on 16 sts. K every row until the length of the piece measures the same as the width (about 4½ inches). Bind off.

This is the same square that you made for the sample. You will get three of these from one ounce of yarn. A four-ounce skein will make twelve or thirteen.

Pincushion

Use two squares of different colors that look good together. Arrange squares as shown (*a*), so knitting

(*a*)

will not stretch in one direction, and pin together evenly along three sides. Sew along the three sides. Stuff the pincushion with old nylon stockings or clean rags that have been cut into small pieces. Foam rubber is also very good and can be bought already cut up (b). Sew up the remaining side.

(b)

Put fringe on the corners, following directions on page 33. Cut the fringe 6 inches long. You will need four pieces of fringe for each corner, two of each color. Attach to corners of pincushion with crochet hook, using all four pieces at the same time (c).

(c)

Pillow (2 Squares)

Follow directions for pincushion, but cast on 32 sts. The squares will be about 9 inches × 9 inches. Make the fringe 7 inches long and use eight pieces on each corner, four of each color, following directions for fringe on page 33.

Pillows: two squares (left), eight squares (right).

Pillow (8 Squares)

Follow directions for making squares on page 38. Using two colors of yarn, make four squares of each color. Sew four squares together to form each side, arranging colors and direction of knitting as shown. Make the fringe 7 inches long and use eight pieces on each corner, four of each color, following directions for fringe on page 33.

An attractive addition is fringe along the seams. Pieces should be 5 inches long. Use two pieces at a time, one of each color. Use your own ideas for other decoration for the pillows.

Afghan (Blanket)

For an afghan that measure 36 inches × 50 inches you will need 88 squares. Make squares following the directions on page 38. This is a good way to use up small amounts of wool of different colors. Many attractive color combinations are possible.

An afghan may be any size you want. Lay your squares out on the floor to get an idea of the size, and knit more squares if it does not seem large enough.

Sew squares together following directions for sewing on page 32. Arrange squares so direction of knit-

ting changes, as shown. Use yarn of one color to sew the squares together. The afghan will be eleven squares long and eight squares wide. You can add fringe if you like.

A good size for a baby blanket would be 32 inches × 40 inches. This will need sixty-three squares (nine squares long and seven squares wide). Pastel (light) colors make a pretty baby blanket.

STRIPED AFGHAN

Knitting needles	1 pair size 10½
Yarn	24 to 28 oz (4-ply)
Size	40 in × 58 in

Another style of afghan that is a good way to use up leftover yarn (or new yarn of different colors) is a striped afghan. The choice of colors and the size of

the stripes are up to you. Stripes about five rows wide are attractive, and stripes of different widths make an interesting pattern.

For an afghan 40 inches wide, cast on 140 sts. K a few rows, and then start with a new color, joining yarn at the end of the row as described on page 37. Knit until afghan is the size that you want.

A small striped afghan in pastel colors makes a nice baby blanket.

SHOULDER BAG

Knitting needles	1 pair size 10½
Yarn	4 oz (4-ply)
Size (flat)	11 in × 24 in
Size (folded)	11 in × 12 in

Cast on 40 sts. K every row for 24 inches. Bind off. *Shoulder strap:* Cast on 5 sts. K every row for 30 inches. Bind off.

To put bag together: Block large piece, following directions on page 59. Attach lining, if you wish, following directions below.

Fold bag in half and pin sides together neatly. Sew seams from the outside (right side), following directions on page 32. Turn a small hem to the wrong side all along the top. Sew this neatly.

Pin the shoulder strap to the sides, letting 5 inches at each end of strap extend down 5 inches along side seam. Sew along both sides of strap and across bottom, and fasten yarn well.

The top of the bag may be left open, or it may be closed with a zipper, a snap, or a button and loop (page 46). Fringe may be added to the bottom of the bag.

LINING: If a lining is used the bag will be firmer and will not stretch. The easiest kind of lining to use is an iron-on lining. You may buy different kinds of iron-on fabric in a five-and-ten or department store.

To line this bag, cut lining a little bit smaller than the flat knitted piece. After the knitting has been blocked, leave it pinned to the ironing board. Pin the lining to the knitting, shiny side down, with the pins sticking into the ironing board to hold pieces firmly. Use a pressing cloth when you press on the lining. You may have to rest the iron on the cloth to make the lining stick well.

PURSE

Knitting needles	1 pair size 10½
Yarn	2 oz (4-ply)
Size (flat)	8½ in × 14½ in
Size (folded)	8½ in × 6 in

Cast on 30 sts. K until piece measures 14½ inches. Bind off. *Handle:* Cast on 4 sts. K until piece measures 20 inches. Bind off.

To put purse together: Block large piece, following directions on page 59. Follow the directions on page 44 if lining is to be used. Lining will keep purse from stretching out of shape.

Fold knitted piece about 5 inches from one end.

(a)

This will leave about 4 inches to extend at the top (a). Pin edges of folded part together and sew neatly, following directions for sewing on page 32. Sew from the outside (right side).

Pin 2 inches of each end of handle over top 2 inches of side seams. Sew neatly around bottom and sides of handle end.

To fasten purse with button and loop, follow directions below.

TO MAKE LOOP FOR BUTTON: Measure flap of purse to find the center. Mark this with a pin.

Thread tapestry needle with the same yarn you used for the purse. At one side of center pin, take a few small stitches to fasten end of yarn (b). Instead of pulling the last stitch tight, leave a loop about an inch long (c). Reach through the loop, grab the loose part

(b)

(c)

(f)

of the yarn with your fingers, and pull through to make another loop. Pull it firmly so the first loop is pulled tight (d). Keep doing this to form a chain. When chain is long enough to go around button, finish it by putting needle through last loop and pulling it tight (e). Fasten to purse on the other side of center pin by taking a few stitches (f). Sew on button.

GARTER STITCH HAT

Knitting needles	1 pair size 10½
Yarn	2½ oz (4-ply)

Cast on 68 sts. K every row until piece measures 8 inches. (If you would like a longer hat, just knit 1 or 2 inches more.)

Leave the stitches on the needle and cut the yarn, leaving 20 inches attached to the knitting. Thread this end of yarn through a tapestry needle and draw the tapestry needle through the stitches (*a*). Remove knitting needle (*b*). Pull the yarn tightly and fasten by sewing a few stitches into the hat with it.

Pin the side seam together evenly and sew with this

(a)

same yarn. At the end of the seam fasten yarn well
and hide the end by weaving it into a few nearby
stitches.

(b)

POMPON: Take a piece of cardboard about 2 inches wide and wind the yarn around it about one hundred times. Cut a piece of yarn 10 inches long. Put it under the yarn on the cardboard as shown (a). Remove yarn from cardboard and tie the 10-inch piece tightly around it, using three or four good knots (b). Cut the ends of the loops open (c). You now have a pompon.

Thread the ends of the 10-inch piece into a tapestry needle and use this to sew pompon securely to the top of the hat. If the ends of the pompon are uneven they may be trimmed with scissors.

STOCKINETTE STITCH HAT

Knitting needles   1 pair size 10½
Yarn   2 oz (4-ply)

Cast on 62 sts. K one row, p one row for 7½ inches. Leave the stitches on the needle and follow the directions for the hat on page 50. Follow the directions for the pompon on page 52.

This stitch (knitting one row, purling one row) is called *stockinette stitch*. The side that shows when you are knitting, which is the right side, looks different from the side that shows when you are purling. The bottom of this hat is turned up to show the wrong side. Directions for purling are given on the next page.

HOW TO PURL: The purl stitch is made like the knit stitch, except that the needle goes through the stitch from back to front instead of from front to back. Follow the directions under the pictures and do one step at a time.

1. Hold needles as you do for knitting. Put right needle through first stitch from back to front.

2. Using your right hand, pick up the yarn from the front and bring it over and around the right needle.

3. Hold the yarn and the right needle with your right hand, pulling yarn firmly against right needle.

4. Use the right needle to pull the yarn through the loop.

5. Slip the new stitch off the left needle.

RIBBED HAT

Knitting needles   1 pair size 10½
Yarn   2 oz (4-ply)

Cast on 62 sts. K1, p1 every row for 7½ inches. This stitch is called *ribbing*. Follow directions on page 50 for putting the hat together. Follow directions for pompon on page 52.

HOW TO DO RIBBING: Knit the first stitch, purl the second stitch (see directions for purling on page 54), knit the third stitch, purl the fourth stitch, and so on. Note that you must bring the yarn *toward you* before every purl stitch, in order to have it in front, and *back away from you* before every knit stitch. Your stitches should make straight lines, like those in the picture. With an even number of stitches, start every row with k 1. Ribbing is more elastic (stretchy) than garter stitch or stockinette stitch. It looks the same on both sides.

how to care for knitted articles

WASHING

Wash knits made with woolen yarn in cold water with a mild detergent or soap. Rinse several times in cold water. Squeeze gently to remove all suds. Squeeze as dry as you can but *do not wring*.

Lay the article flat on a bath towel. Starting at one end, roll the towel up loosely. Press on it to squeeze out the extra water. Now unroll and lay article out flat on a dry towel, away from heat. Always put knits on a flat surface to dry. If you hang them, they will stretch. Woolen garments that are dried in the sun will fade, so dry them indoors.

Knits made from synthetic (man-made) yarns such as nylon, Orlon, or Acrilan may be washed in the washing machine.

BLOCKING

Blocking is shaping the article to the size that you want while it is wet.

Before you wash your article, measure the length and the width and write the measurements down, or

59

trace the outline of the article on a piece of paper. After it is washed you can easily shape it to the same measurements or to fit the tracing. If you would like to make a small change in the measurements you can stretch it wider or longer. Pat and smooth the article gently and allow it to dry. This gives the knitting a nice even look.

Even if the article does not need to be washed, it can be blocked in the same way. Wet it thoroughly in cold water and follow the same directions.

Another way to block knitting is to steam it. Place the knitting flat on the ironing board, wrong side up. Pin it to the ironing board with straight pins. Put a wet pressing cloth on top of it. Any clean cloth may be used for this. Just wet the cloth well and wring out the extra water. Even if you are using a steam iron, use the wet cloth also, as this will give a better result.

Use a warm (not hot) iron, no hotter than the "wool" setting. Hold the iron close to the pressing cloth, but *do not rest the iron on the cloth.* You want to steam the knitting, but *not to press it flat. Never* press knitting with a dry iron.

Allow the knitting to dry before removing the pins. Any marks left by the pins may be steamed out.

WARNING: Be very careful when using an iron as you can get burned. Remember that steam is hotter than dry heat.

Ready-made, machine-knitted articles may be washed and blocked in the same way.

helpful hints

This book has shown the easiest way to knit. There are other ways to cast on stitches, to knit, to hold the needles and the yarn. As you become a more experienced knitter you will develop your own style of knitting.

Keep your work *loose*. It must move along the needles very easily.

You can rest your needles on your lap or on a table when you are learning to knit. Later, when you are more experienced, you may find that you like to hold them a different way.

Finish a row before you stop your knitting. If you stop in the middle of a row, you may make a mistake when you start again by going the wrong way.

When you bind off stitches, keep them loose. An easy way to do this is to use a larger needle when you bind off.

Measure knitting with a ruler or tape measure on a flat surface such as a table or the floor.

Do not expect your knitting to look perfectly even. Hand knitting is never as perfect as knitting that is done by machine. It will look much better after it is blocked.

As you practice you will find that your work will look better. This is because you have learned to pull your yarn evenly.

Keep your knitting and needles in a bag. You may have a knitting bag, or you may use a shopping bag or a heavy plastic bag. The shoulder bag on page 44 is good to use as a knitting bag.

If you are left-handed follow the directions, but when it says "right hand" use your left hand, and when it says "left hand" use your right hand. Use a mirror when you look at the diagrams, and look into the mirror. This will give you the picture for left-handed knitting.

Use only cold water to wash a woolen garment. Never use hot water, which will make your article shrink and fade.

When washing a woolen article, squeeze out the extra water and roll it in a towel. Do not wring, as this will stretch the knitting. Never dry wool in the sun, as it will fade. Keep away from heat when drying indoors.

If you do not have enough yarn of one color, use a combination. Stripes are attractive. Be sure to use the same weight yarn.

Never cut a knitted garment. It will unravel and rip apart. Remember that knitting is made of one long continuous thread.

If you buy your yarn in a knitting shop or a department store, they will give you free instructions. In a department store, this department is called "Art Needlework."

You can find directions for other knitted things in books and pamphlets in knitting shops, department stores, five-and-ten-cent stores, and libraries. Magazines have articles about knitting and have newer styles than books.

glossary

Acrilan	a synthetic (man-made) fiber
blocking	shaping a knitted article
cotton	a fiber made from the cotton plant
dowel	a round wooden stick that can be bought at a hardware store or lumberyard
fiber	tiny, fine threads that are twisted together to form thread for sewing and yarn for knitting. These may be cotton, wool, or synthetic
nylon	a synthetic (man-made) fiber
Orlon	a synthetic (man-made) fiber
ply	a strand of thread that is twisted together with other threads to form yarn for knitting
rip	to pull knitting apart
sandpaper	strong paper coated with sand, used for smoothing and polishing wood
skein	a coil of yarn
stitch	in knitting, a loop of yarn (as in "knit stitch") or the pattern made by the loops (as in "garter stitch")
tapestry needle	large needle with blunt end and large eye
thread	twisted fibers of any kind
unravel	to pull knitting apart
wool	anything made of the fibers from the fleece of sheep
yarn	thread made by twisting strands (ply) together, used for knitting or weaving